The
WILDLIFE ADVENTURE
Creativity Book

Open up and take a look
At nature's secrets in this book!
Join the fun, with things to do,
Games to play, and stickers, too!

This Creativity Book
belongs to

....

BARRON'S

What's Inside This Book?

INVENTIVE FUN!

There are lots of pages where you can write, draw, and color. This book will end up being made mostly by you!

THINGS TO MAKE

Make your own butterflies on page 14 and create your own glowing desert night picture on page 22. There's a 3-D ocean to make on page 56 and a "grow your own art" project on page 72. On pages 28 and 29, there's some art paper to use in your art projects, too.

STICKERS

There are sticker sheets at the back of this book along with two fold-out sticker scenes of an ocean and a rain forest. Use your stickers to decorate the scenes, your pencil case, or anything else you like.

STENCILS

Carefully pull the sheet of stencils out of your book. You can use it on some of the pages here and on your own art, too.

PUZZLES AND GAMES

Connect the dots, follow mixed-up paths, and match pictures as you work through your book. There's even a game to play based on racing to the North Pole.

First edition for North America published in 2013 by Barron's Educational Series, Inc. Text, design, and illustration copyright © Carlton Books 2012

Published in 2012 by Carlton Books Limited, an imprint of the Carlton Publishing Group, 20 Mortimer Street, London, W1T 3JW.

All inquiries should be addressed to: Barron's Educational Series, Inc. 250 Wireless Boulevard Hauppauge, NY 11788 www.barronseduc.com

ISBN: 978-1-4380-0241-5

Library of Congress Control Number: 2012943880

Date of Manufacture: November 2012 Manufactured by: Hung Hing Offset Printing Co., Ltd., Shenzhen, China

Product conforms to all applicable CPSC and CPSIA 2008 standards. No lead or phthalate hazard.

Printed in China
9 8 7 6 5 4 3 2 1

AUTHOR: Moira Butterfield
PUBLISHER: Sam Sweeney
CREATIVE DIRECTOR: Clare Baggaley
SENIOR EDITOR: Anna Bowles
COVER DESIGN: Emily Clarke
DESIGN: Ceri Hurst
ILLUSTRATIONS: Nicola O'Byrne
PRODUCTION: Claire Halligan

PICTURE CREDITS

The publishers thank the following sources for their kind permission to reproduce the pictures in this book:

Key, t=top, l=left, r=right, c=center, b=bottom.

Alamy Images: /Classic Image: 7; Getty Images: 39tr, 52tr, 70br; iStockphoto.com: 15tr, 17tl, 20tr, 27tr, 40bl, 41tr; NASA: /hubblesite.org: 17bl; Science Photo Library: /Power & Syred: 52l, /Dr. Wolf Fahrenbach/ Visuals Unlimited: 52r; Shutterstock.com: 35tr, 68bl; Thinkstockphotos.com: 11, 16bl, 30tr, 30c, 41t, 42tr, 43, 52bl, 52br, 60; Stickers: iStockphoto.com, Shutterstock.com, Thinkstockphotos.com.

Every effort has been made to acknowledge correctly and contact the source and/ or copyright holder of each picture, and Carlton Books Limited apologizes for any unintentional errors or omissions, which will be corrected in future editions of this book.

Calling All Explorers!

Imagine you are applying to join an exciting expedition to discover the secrets of the natural world.

CHECK THE USEFUL SKILLS YOU HAVE.

- ☐ I'm good at helping others.
- ☐ I can cook some food.
- ☐ I can swim.
- ☐ I can walk a long way.
- ☐ I'm good at climbing.
- ☐ I can read a map.
- ☐ I can read a compass.
- ☐ I can sleep in a sleeping bag.

Exploring Starts Here

Here are six important natural areas of the world that you'll be exploring in this book. Finish coloring them in and choose the one you would like to visit.

THE POLES: The far north and south of the world, where it is very cold and icy. If you went north you might see a polar bear.

RAIN FOREST: The jungles of the world provide a home for many animals, including frogs, monkeys, and parrots.

DESERT: The driest places in the world. The biggest one is the Sahara in Africa, where you might see camels trekking across the sand.

GRASSLAND: The giant grassy plains of the world, where animals graze. On African grasslands you would find zebras munching the grass.

NORTHERN FOREST (also called the taiga): Fir-tree forests cover a vast stretch of the northern world. Here you will find wild bears hunting for food.

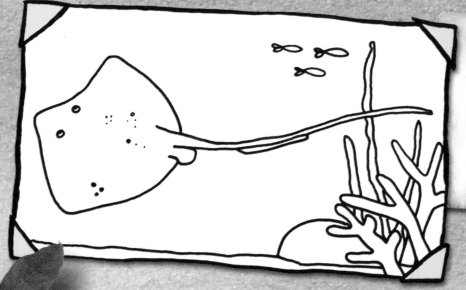

THE OCEANS: Oceans cover 70% of the world, providing a home for all kinds of sea creatures.

I WOULD LIKE TO VISIT ....

5

Make Sure Nothing Goes Wrong!

An expedition to explore the natural world needs careful planning if you don't want to get lost down the wrong path with nothing but a pair of flip-flops and a piece of chewing gum! Here's the place to make the perfect plan.

I am going to ....

What I want to find:

☐ A new type of insect

☐ A new type of bird

☐ A new type of fish

☐ A new type of plant

People I would take on my expedition:

1. ....

2. ....

3. ....

4. ....

All Geared Up

Choosing the right equipment is
vital for an expedition into the wild.

Check one item that you would like to take from each list.

BEST VEHICLE

- [ ] Truck
- [ ] Bicycle
- [ ] Helicopter
- [ ] Boat

BEST CLOTHING

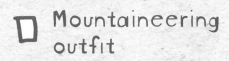

- [ ] Mountaineering outfit
- [ ] Diving outfit
- [ ] Jungle outfit
- [ ] Polar outfit

BEST HI-TECH GADGET

- [ ] Animal tracking equipment
- [ ] Animal sound recorder
- [ ] Underwater camera
- [ ] Night-vision goggles

VITAL SUPPLIES:

You would definitely need to pack these things for a trip into the wild. Check what you already have at home.

- [ ] Sunhat
- [ ] Sunscreen
- [ ] Waterproof top
- [ ] Sleeping bag
- [ ] Tent
- [ ] Backpack
- [ ] Walking boots
- [ ] Flashlight
- [ ] Watch
- [ ] Compass
- [ ] Adhesive bandages
- [ ] Insect repellent

My Map

Draw an imaginary map of a place you would like to visit to discover a new animal or plant. Label things like mountains, rivers, lakes, and towns.

SOME FEATURES
YOU COULD INCLUDE:

Jungle
Desert
Fir-tree forest
Snowy mountains
Volcano
Lake
Swamp
River
Waterfall
Caves
Beaches

THIS PLACE IS CALLED ···

My Expedition Badge

Design an official badge for your expedition T-shirt. You could use your stencils and stickers to decorate it, if you like.

Decorate this expedition vehicle, so that it looks right for a trip to the wild. You might want to give it zebra stripes or camouflage, for instance. Check out your art paper on pages 28 and 29 for ideas.

Discover the Rain Forests

The rain forests are home to over
half of the world's plants and animals.

Color in this map of the Earth's rain forest areas.
They are marked with the letter R. Color them green
and make the rest of the map a different color.

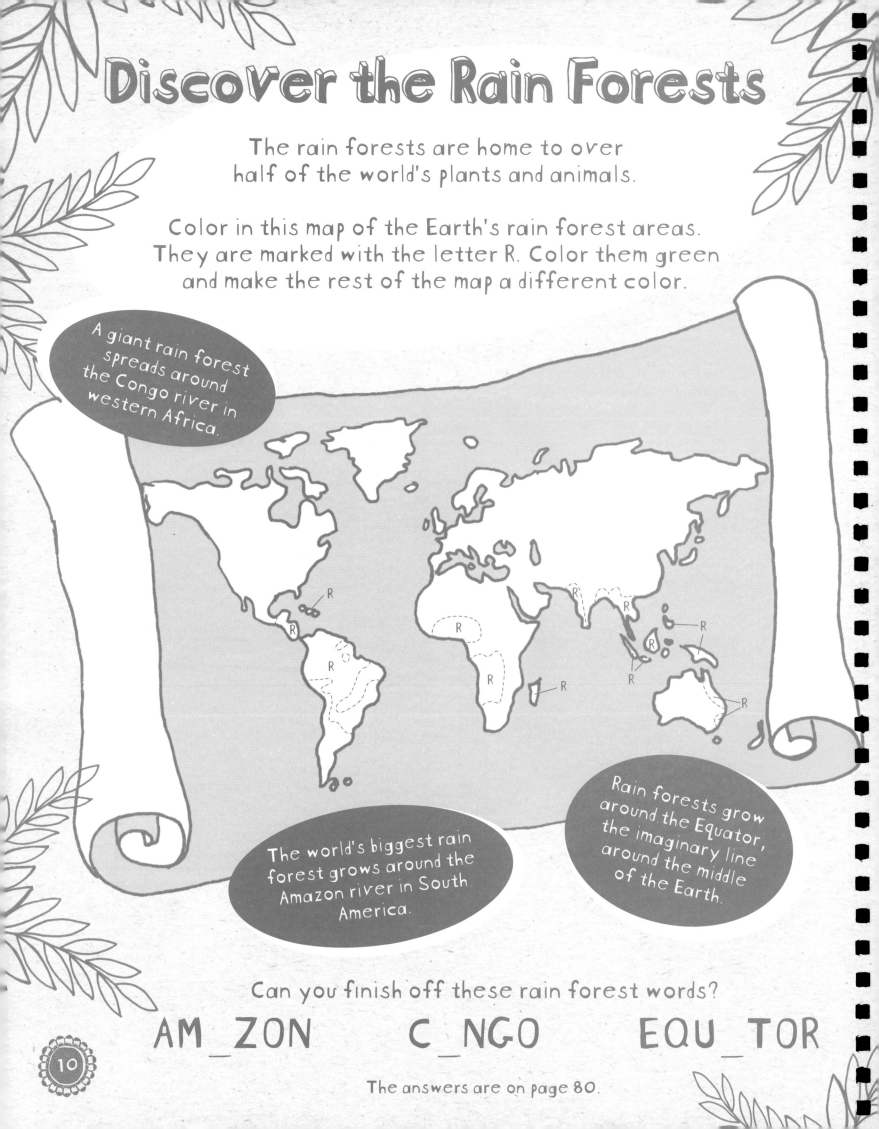

A giant rain forest
spreads around
the Congo river in
western Africa.

The world's biggest rain
forest grows around the
Amazon river in South
America.

Rain forests grow
around the Equator,
the imaginary line
around the middle
of the Earth.

Can you finish off these rain forest words?

AM_ZON   C_NGO   EQU_TOR

10

The answers are on page 80.

Are You Ready for the Rain Forest?

Try this rain forest quiz.

Be warned... Some of the questions are tricky! Make a good guess at the ones you don't know.

1. It rains a lot in a rain forest.   True / False

2. The weather there is always warm.   True / False

3. Animals don't like living in rain forests.   True / False

4. You might see a polar bear in a rain forest.   True / False

5. You might see a parrot in a rain forest.   True / False

6. It never gets dark in a rain forest.   True / False

7. There are four different types of trees in a rain forest.   True / False

8. Rain forest flowers are all red.   True / False

NOW TURN TO PAGE 80 AND LOOK AT THE ANSWERS. HOW DID YOU DO?

MORE THAN 5—Well done! You are an ideal rain forest explorer.

BETWEEN 3 AND 5—Not bad, but find out some more facts before you venture into the jungle.

LESS THAN 3—You definitely need to read up on rain forests before you ever go there. Otherwise you might get a shock!

MY SCORE

Meet the Rain Forest Animals

Color in this Amazon rain forest tree full of animals.

Fill the numbered shapes with their matching colors.
1 – Gray
2 – Blue
3 – Red
4 – Yellow
5 – Green
6 – Brown
7 – Black

Once you have finished the picture, shut the book for a moment and see how many of the animals you can remember.

TOUCAN

SNAKE

MACAW

SLOTH

BUTTERFLY

COLOBUS MONKEY

SPIDER MONKEY

The world's rain forests are disappearing because they are being cut down for their wood or to make farmland.

Finish coloring in this campaign poster to help save them. You could use stencils to decorate it.

SAVE OUR RAIN FORESTS

YOU CAN HELP BY MAKING SURE YOUR FAMILY ONLY BUYS WOOD PRODUCTS THAT ARE MARKED AS FOREST-FRIENDLY.

IF THE RAIN FORESTS DISAPPEAR, SO WILL MANY OF THE WORLD'S ANIMALS AND PLANTS.

Make Your Own Butterflies

The largest butterflies in the world live in the rain forests.

On the next few pages there are two beautiful ones to make and pop onto their own stands.

1. Carefully CUT out pages 15 to 18.

2. CUT along the dotted lines so that you have two butterflies and two butterfly stands.

3. COLOR in the backs of your butterflies however you like.

4. To make a stand, CUT along the solid lines in the center to make a little flap. Fold the stand in half, with the flap sticking up.

5. Carefully CUT along the solid lines to make a slit in the base of each butterfly. Slot the butterflies onto the top of the stands.

Morpho Butterfly
from South America

It can grow up to 8 in (20 cm) wide.

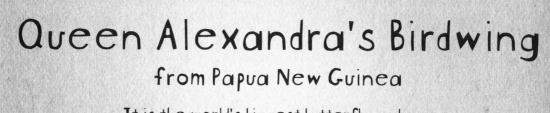

Queen Alexandra's Birdwing
from Papua New Guinea

It is the world's biggest butterfly and can
grow up to 1 ft (30 cm) wide.

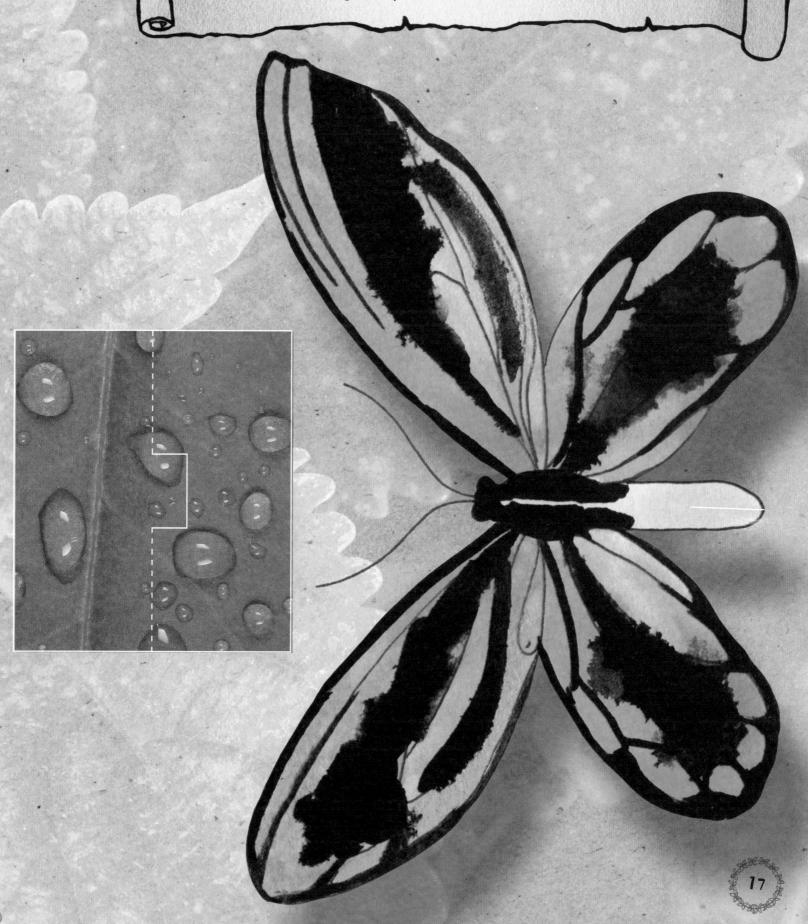

World's Weirdest Plant

The tropical rain forests are full of wonderful plants, and there are thought to be many that are still undiscovered. Draw your own imaginary rain forest plant here, and write about it, too.

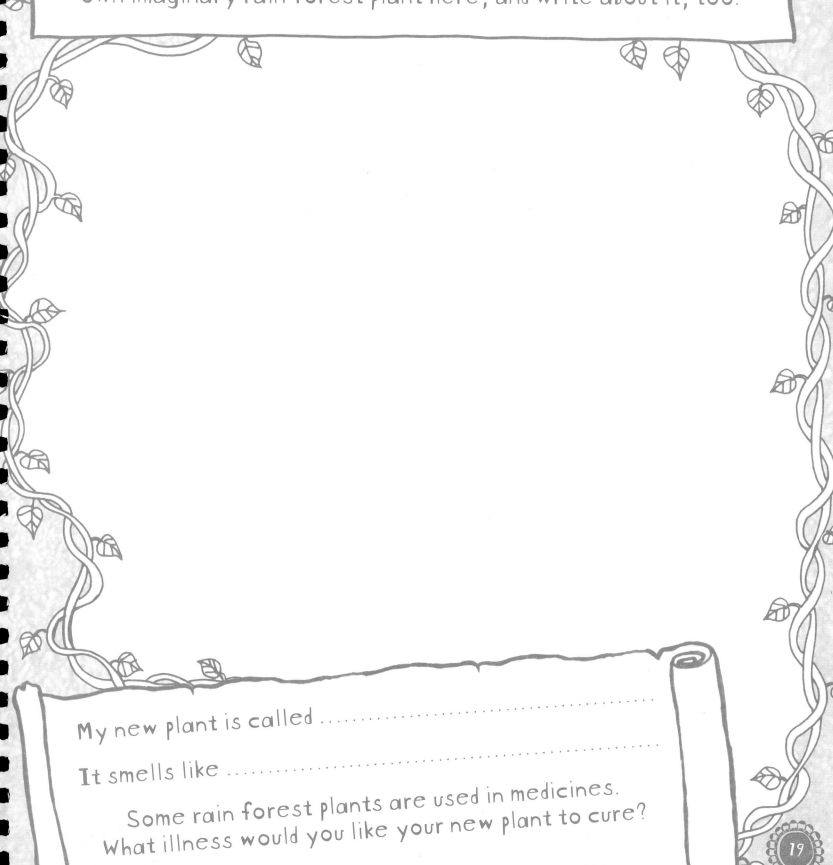

My new plant is called ....

It smells like ....

Some rain forest plants are used in medicines.
What illness would you like your new plant to cure?

Be a Plant Hunter

Follow the secret jungle paths to find out about some unusual rain forest plants.

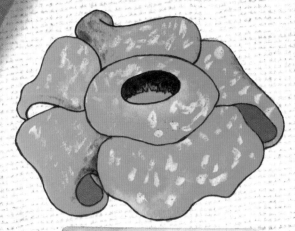

RAFFLESIA ARNOLDII

BROMELIAD

JUNGLE ORCHIDS

The rarest and most expensive flowers in the world. Orchid hunters will brave great danger to find unusual ones.

Bromeliads grow high in the sky, on rain forest tree branches. Their roots collect water by dangling in the air.

The largest flower on Earth grows up to 3 ft (1 m) wide in the jungles of Sumatra in Southeast Asia. It has an awful smell, like rotting meat.

DID YOU KNOW?

In the 1800s many orchid hunters risked death to find valuable plants. They faced wild animals, disease, floods, earthquakes, and even cannibals to try to make their fortune.

The answers are on page 80.

Explore the Desert

The world's deserts are the driest places on Earth, but there are animals tough enough to live there.

Connect the dots to find some of them.

The shy little desert cat lives in the deserts of the Middle East. It only comes out at night.

Scorpions live in African and American deserts. The tip of a scorpion's tail carries a painful sting.

DID YOU KNOW?
The world's biggest desert is the Sahara in North Africa. It stretches for 3.5 million square miles (9 million square km). Its vast empty regions have very little water, and few people live there.

The answers are on page 80.

21

Desert Night

Make a dramatic picture of a desert night by pricking lots of small holes through paper, then taping your picture where light will shine through it at night.

1. Carefully cut out the nighttime picture page.

2. Use easy-to-remove masking tape to anchor the picture onto some thick cardboard. Corrugated cardboard is best, or cardboard from a thick box. It will protect the table while you make your picture.

3. Use a pushpin to gently prick holes in the paper, along the lines of the picture. Make the holes far enough apart so they don't connect. The more holes there are, the more light will show through.

4. If you like, you can tape colored tissue paper onto the back of your picture. Then when light shines through the holes, they will be colored.

5. Tape your picture to a window, where light will shine through the picture from behind.

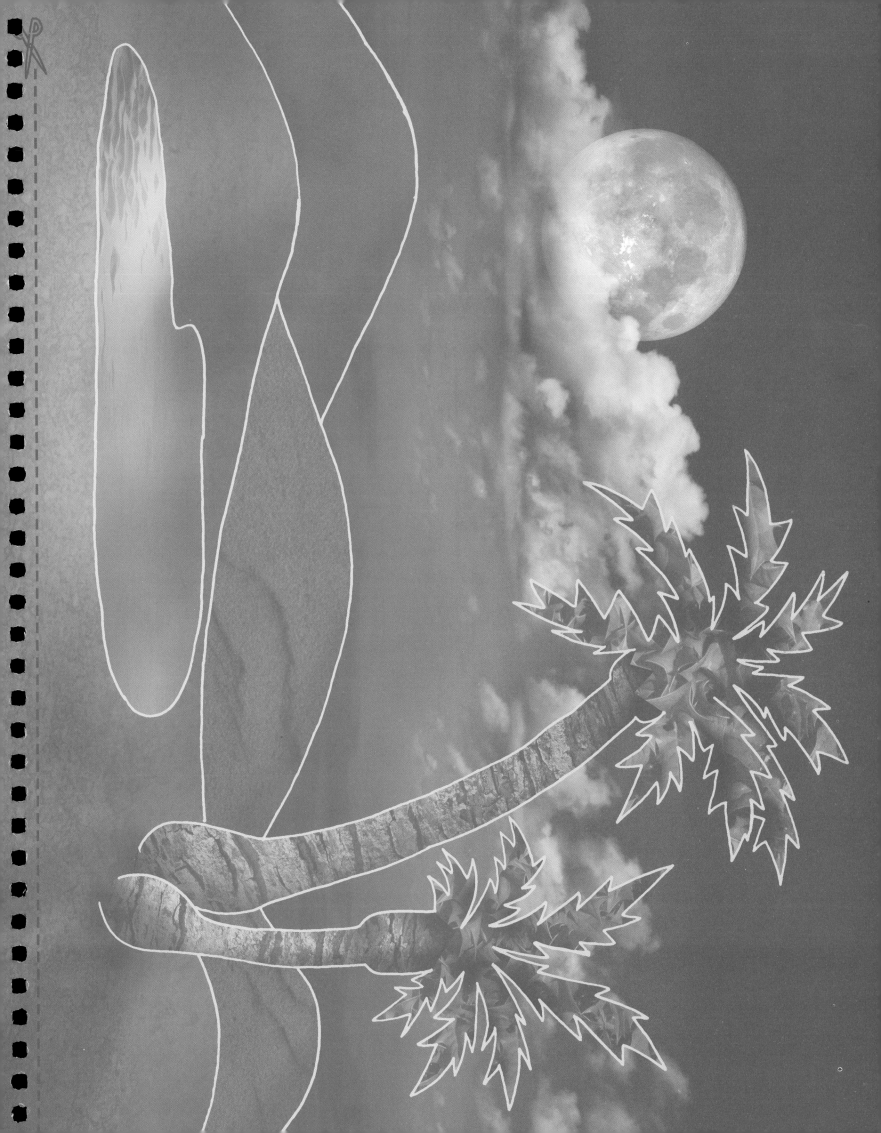

Grassland Trek

Grasslands are wide grassy plains that cover about a quarter of the Earth. They make a good home for animals that graze on grass, and for animals that hunt the grazers. About half of Africa is covered by grassland called savanna.

Find your way through the savanna maze, avoiding the lion, the rhino, and the snake!

START

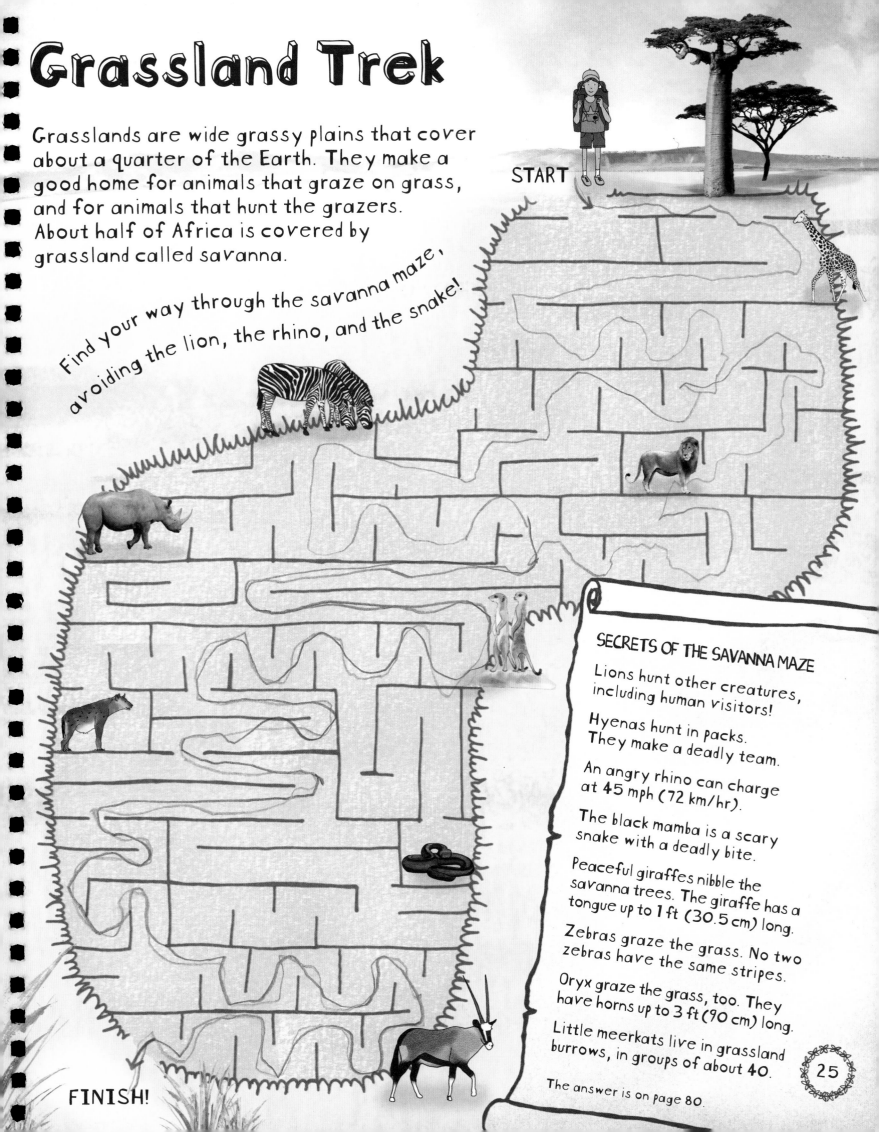

SECRETS OF THE SAVANNA MAZE

Lions hunt other creatures, including human visitors!

Hyenas hunt in packs. They make a deadly team.

An angry rhino can charge at 45 mph (72 km/hr).

The black mamba is a scary snake with a deadly bite.

Peaceful giraffes nibble the savanna trees. The giraffe has a tongue up to 1 ft (30.5 cm) long.

Zebras graze the grass. No two zebras have the same stripes.

Oryx graze the grass, too. They have horns up to 3 ft (90 cm) long.

Little meerkats live in grassland burrows, in groups of about 40.

FINISH!

The answer is on page 80.

Camouflage Creator

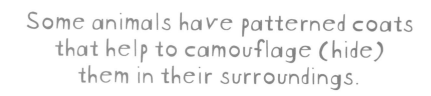

Some animals have patterned coats that help to camouflage (hide) them in their surroundings.

Cut out these super-cool animal camouflage papers to decorate your wildlife art projects.

Art Paper Ideas

Use your stencils to draw shapes on the back of your art paper. Carefully cut the shapes out and stick them wherever you like. They make great decoration for notebook covers!

Cool collage—Create a wildlife collage picture.

1. Begin by using your stencils to draw animal outlines, and add some background scenery lines.

2. Once you've planned your picture, cut out color snippets from old magazines and glue them on to build up the color. Add snippets of your art paper, too.

Animal Artist Zone

Draw this cute little savanna elephant in pencil first.
Then go around the outline in color and erase the pencil marks.

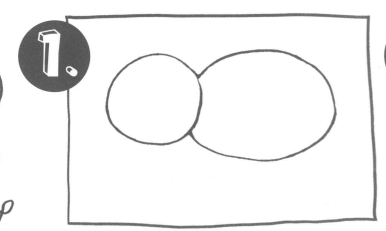

Draw a circle for the head
and an oval for the body.

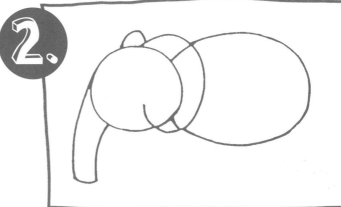

Add a trunk and two ears.

Add four legs, some
elephant toes, and a tail.

Then add an eye, a mouth, and
some wrinkle lines on the trunk.

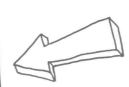

Draw your
elephant here.

MY ELEPHANT IS NAMED

. . . .

African Safari

Tourists are on safari in the African savanna.
Use your stencils to add animals and plants for them to see.

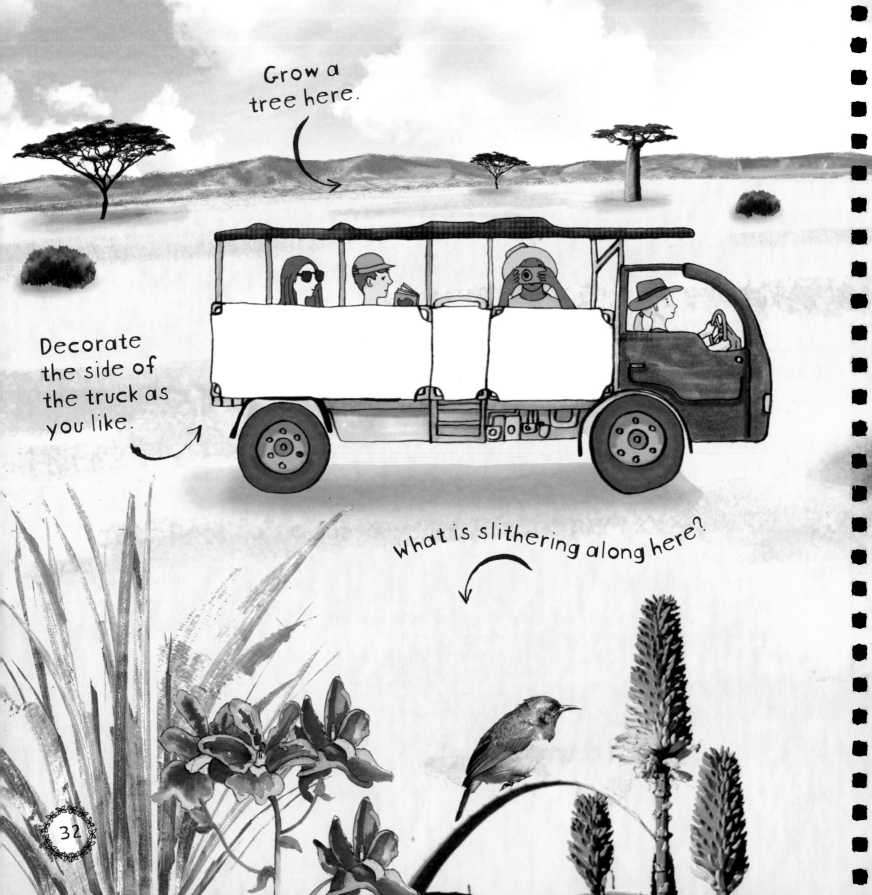

Grow a tree here.

Decorate the side of the truck as you like.

What is slithering along here?

Reach the Poles!

The poles are found at the top and bottom of the Earth. They are very cold places, too icy for plants to grow. Only a few animals make these chilly regions their home.

Nobody lives at the poles, but people visit.

North Pole

These animals live in the Arctic, the far north of the world around the North Pole. Can you connect the facts to the animal shapes?

It is dark for six months of the year at the North and South Poles.

South Pole

A. This giant white bear has paws the size of dinner plates and can stand on its strong hind legs.

B. This beautiful bird glides softly down on its wide wings to grab little creatures in its claws.

C. This sea animal swims in the icy Arctic sea, looking for fish to eat.

D. This furry little fox sometimes wraps its bushy tail around its face to keep warm when it is sleeping.

The answers are on page 80.

Pencil Penguin

Penguins live in the Antarctic, the far south of the world around the South Pole.

Copy each step-by-step picture to draw your own cute penguin.

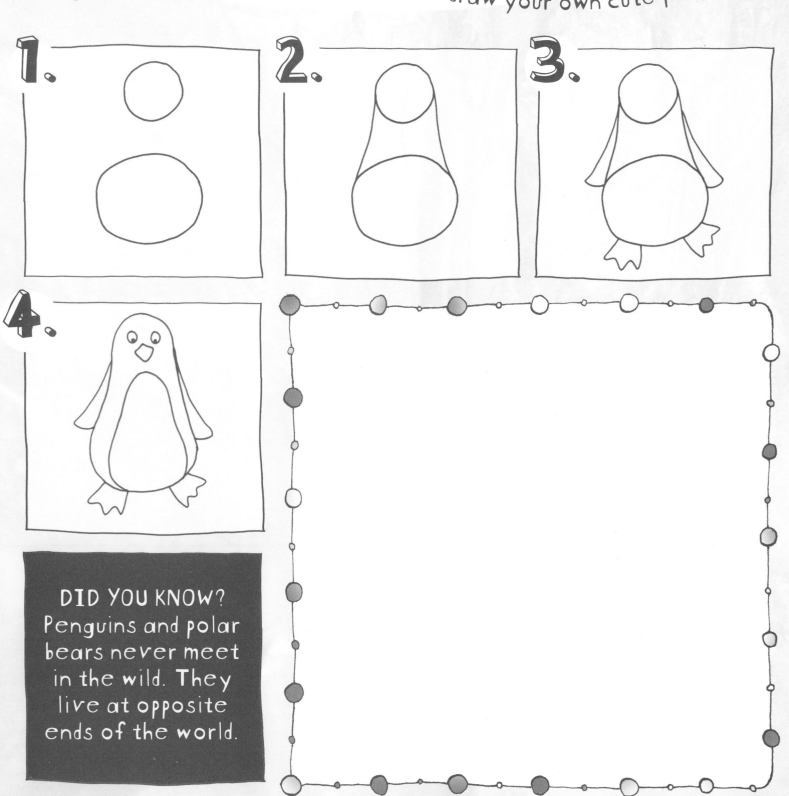

1.

2.

3.

4.

DID YOU KNOW? Penguins and polar bears never meet in the wild. They live at opposite ends of the world.

MY PENGUIN'S NAME IS ....

Arctic Photo Adventure

Race across the snowy Arctic wastes taking photos as you go. Who will finish their journey first?

HOW TO PLAY

❄ This is a game for two or more players.

❄ You need a die, and a counter for each player.

❄ Take turns to roll the die, then move your counter along the track, following any instructions you land on.

❄ The winner is the first player to reach the North Pole.

5 YOU ARE CHASED BY A POLAR BEAR! GO BACK ONE SPACE.

24 YOU CATCH A HELICOPTER. GO STRAIGHT TO THE NORTH POLE!

4

23 YOU GET FROSTBITE ON YOUR TOES. MISS A TURN.

6 YOU TAKE A BRILLIANT PHOTO OF A SNOWY OWL. MOVE FORWARD THREE SPACES.

3 YOU MUST SHELTER FROM A SNOWSTORM! MISS A TURN.

2 YOU CHASE A FAST ARCTIC FOX AND GET A GREAT PHOTO. MOVE FORWARD TWO SPACES.

7

1

8 DISASTER! YOU DROP YOUR CAMERA IN THE ICY ARCTIC OCEAN. GO BACK TO THE BEGINNING.

START

9

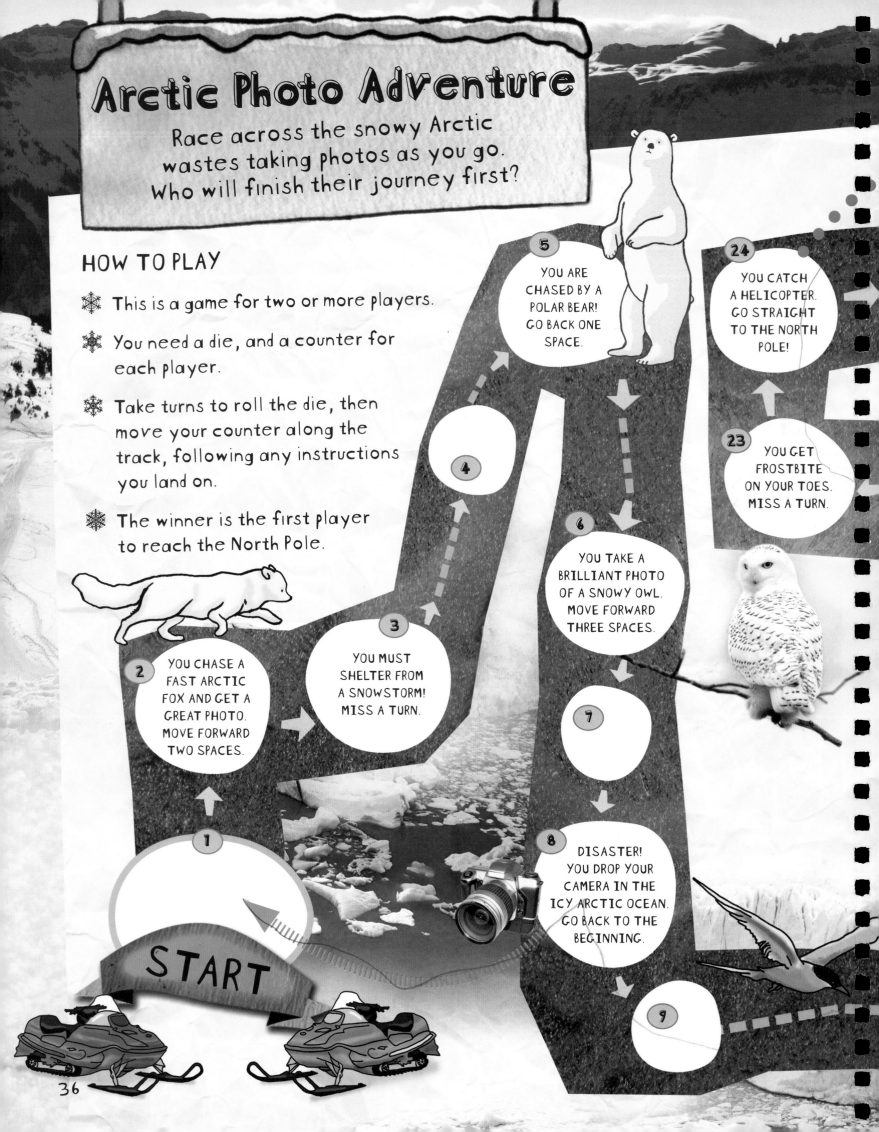

THE NORTH POLE

CONGRATULATIONS TO THE FIRST ARRIVAL!

FINISH!

25 YOU HAVE TO WAIT A LONG TIME TO TAKE A PHOTO OF AN ARCTIC HARE. MISS A TURN.

26

27

22 THE SEA ICE IS BREAKING UP, BLOCKING YOUR PATH. MISS A TURN.

21 YOU MEET SOME LOCAL INUIT PEOPLE, WHO GUIDE YOU VIA A SHORTCUT. GO FORWARD FIVE SPACES.

20

19 YOU SEE SOME BEAUTIFUL BARNACLE GEESE OVERHEAD. GO FORWARD ONE SPACE.

12 YOU ARE KEPT AWAKE IN THE NIGHT BY HOWLING WOLVES. BACK THREE SPACES.

13 YOU SHOOT SOME FANTASTIC VIDEO OF BABY POLAR BEARS PLAYING. GO FORWARD THREE SPACES.

14

15 A HERD OF MUSK OXEN BLOCKS YOUR WAY. MISS A TURN.

18 YOU CRASH YOUR SNOWMOBILE! GO BACK FOUR SPACES.

11

10 YOU SPOT A ...E BABY SEAL. ...FORWARD O... ...ACE.

16

17

Tour the Forest

A huge belt of fir forest stretches across the northern world, in parts of Russia, Scandinavia, and North America.

Color in this picture by the numbers and you will find two animals who live there.

1 - Brown
2 - Dark green
3 - Light green
4 - Blue
5 - Gray

Top Tracker

Which northern forest animals have been out and about in the snow today?

Match the tracks to the animals.

The answers are on page 80.

Artist at Work

The natural world has always been a wonderful inspiration for artists.

Here are some tips for doing great landscapes that look 3-D.

1. Start with a horizon line two-thirds of the way up the page. You could do some overlapping hill lines as shown.

2. Draw big objects at the front and smaller ones at the back, like trees and rocks.

3. Add a winding path that starts off wide at the front and gets narrower as it reaches the horizon line.

4. When you color in your picture, make the colors at the front stronger than the colors at the back.

A German artist named Caspar David Friedrich is famous for his paintings of fir forests and mountains.

Take a look at his work online to inspire you.

40

A Fine Frame

Cut out this frame and stick
it on top of a picture that you
have made of an animal,
plant, or landscape.

Carefully trim around the edges
if your picture sticks out
under the frame.

How to Make Your Picture Frame

1. Carefully CUT this picture frame page out of your book.

2. GLUE the frame onto a piece of cardboard (color side face up).

3. When it's dry, ask a grown-up to help you CUT OUT the finished cardboard frame, both inside and out.

4. Glue the frame over one of your pictures to make it look like it's in a GALLERY!

5. Don't forget to give your beautifully framed picture an artistic TITLE.

A Bad Day in the Forest

Color in this cartoon strip of a forest picnic going wrong and write some words in the speech bubbles.

Treetop Trek

Use stickers to finish this picture of a walkway high up in the treetops. What birds do you think the walkers can see in the trees?

Be a Birdspotter

There's a rare forest bird in this tree and lots of birdwatchers have arrived to watch it.

What do you think it looks like?

Draw it and give it a name.

This rare bird is called a

....

Magic Re-sssss-ycled Snake

Here's an idea for a dancing snake puppet you can make by recycling toilet paper roll tubes.

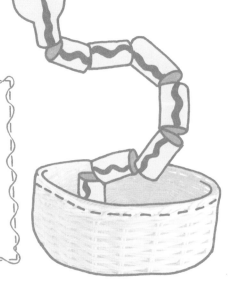

WHAT YOU NEED

5 or 6 empty toilet paper roll tubes

Paint and a paintbrush

A blob of sticky putty

A glue stick

A piece of string about 16 in (about 40 cm) long

A container such as a basket or a cardboard box (that you could decorate with paints)

1. Ask an adult to cut the toilet paper tubes in half for you.

2. Carefully cut around the snake's head on page 48.

3. Paint the toilet paper tube a background color and let the paint dry. Then paint on snake stripes or blobs.

4. Once all the paint is dry, glue the snake's head to the top of a toilet paper tube.

5. Use your sticky putty to fix the string to the bottom of the container. Thread the snake sections onto the string, finishing with the head.

6. Charm your snake up from its basket by slowly pulling up the string.

RECYCLING ALL WE CAN HELPS TO SAVE THE RESOURCES FOUND IN THE NATURAL WORLD, SUCH AS WOOD AND FUEL.

Remember to Recycle

It's possible to recycle packaging, plastic, and glass. Check locally how to do it in your area.

My useful stuff!

Keep a USEFUL STUFF box of things you can use when you want to make something.

Egg cartons and cardboard boxes and tubes make great models when they are glued together. Try making a castle, a haunted house, a palace, or a base for a baddie!

Clean can lids make fun badges. Glue a picture on the inside and glue or tape a safety pin on the back.

On the next page there's a poster that you can color and put up in your kitchen.

It will remind everyone to recycle and to save things for your USEFUL STUFF box.

There are lots of great recycling craft ideas for kids online. Ask an adult to help you find a good project.

All About Oceans

The oceans of the world are home to lots of amazing creatures. Finish coloring this beautiful underwater coral reef and do some animal spotting, too.

CAN YOU SPOT: **1.** A spotty moray eel **2.** A black and white zebra angelfish **3.** Pretty seahorses **4.** An orange, black, and white clown fish

The answers are on page 80.

Discover a Shipwreck

Draw your own diver exploring an underwater shipwreck by copying the left-hand picture into the grid on the right.

 Copy the outline one square at a time.
Then color in your masterpiece.

DID YOU KNOW?

Frenchman Jacques Cousteau was one of the world's most famous ocean explorers.
He helped to invent the AquaLung that divers use to breathe oxygen underwater.
He dived from his boat CALYPSO, and made TV shows about his adventures.

Whale Watching

Match up these whales to their images.

THE BELUGA WHALE lives in the Arctic Ocean. It has a domed head and a lovely call that earns it the nickname "the canary of the sea."

THE HUMPBACK WHALE has a rounded back and long knobbly flippers. Its giant tail can grow up to 12 ft (3.6 m) wide.

THE NARWHAL has a long tusk like a unicorn. Male narwhals have the longest tusks, sometimes measuring up to 10 ft (3 m) long.

THE BLUE WHALE is the world's biggest animal. It can grow up to 94 ft (29 m) long.

The answers are on page 80.

Fish Matcher

Can you spot the fish pairs in this busy aquarium shoal?

There are seven pairs to find.

The answers are on page 80.

Which Fish?

Draw and then color in a new type of rare fish yet to be discovered.

This new type of fish is called a

LIEFISH

DID YOU KNOW?
The coelacanth (see-low-canth) is one of the world's rarest fish. It lives in deep water, and until living coelacanths were discovered a few years ago everybody thought they had died out.

A SEA STORY

One day I found a treasure map and I set sail to find a chest of gold coins. On the way I met a sea monster... UADN and found a lightning fish he chased me in the sea.

THE END

3-D Sea

Fold this card to make a 3-D ocean scene. You could display it in your room or write a message on the back and send it to a friend.

1. Carefully cut around the two sections on page 57.

2. Fold the section with the dolphins as shown.

3. Fold the section with the beach as shown.

4. Carefully glue or tape the two sections together along the tab to the left of the dolphins.

My Wildlife Park

Imagine that you owned a wildlife park where people could visit to marvel at the animals and plants.

My wildlife park would be called

....

My fiercest animal would be a

....

My biggest animal would be a

....

My most poisonous animal would be a

....

My smallest animal would be a

....

My noisiest animal would be a

....

My prettiest animal would be a

....

59

Visitors' Guide

Use your stickers to finish this map of a wildlife park.

GORILLA NEST

PENGUIN POND

SNAKE PIT

BAT ZONE

CAMEL FIELD

60

Inside the Aviary

There are often beautiful birds at wildlife parks, inside giant cages called aviaries. Copy the colors of these fantastic birds to create your own aviary.

Visit Soon!

Finish this poster encouraging visitors to your wildlife park.

Add the name of your park here

COME FOR SOME FUN!

Penguin feeding time

......

Today's special café meal

......

Our head keeper is called

......

At 2pm today our head keeper will be talking about

......

HOW TO PLAY

This game is for two or three players.

1. Ask an adult to help you cut out all the game cards.

2. Mix up the cards and lay them all face down on a table.

3. Each player takes a turn to flip over two cards. If they match up, the player wins the card pair and takes another turn.

4. If the cards don't match, turn them back over. Try to remember where they are for another turn.

5. The game ends when all the cards have been matched up in pairs. The winner is the player with the most pairs (though it could be a draw!).

PIRANHA FISH	FISH-EATING BAT	TAMANDUA	EAGLE OWL
AMAZON RAINFOREST	AMAZON RAINFOREST	AMAZON RAINFOREST	NORTHERN FOREST
WEASEL	WILD BOAR	MUSK OXEN	BELUGA WHALE
NORTHERN FOREST	NORTHERN FOREST	ARCTIC	ARCTIC

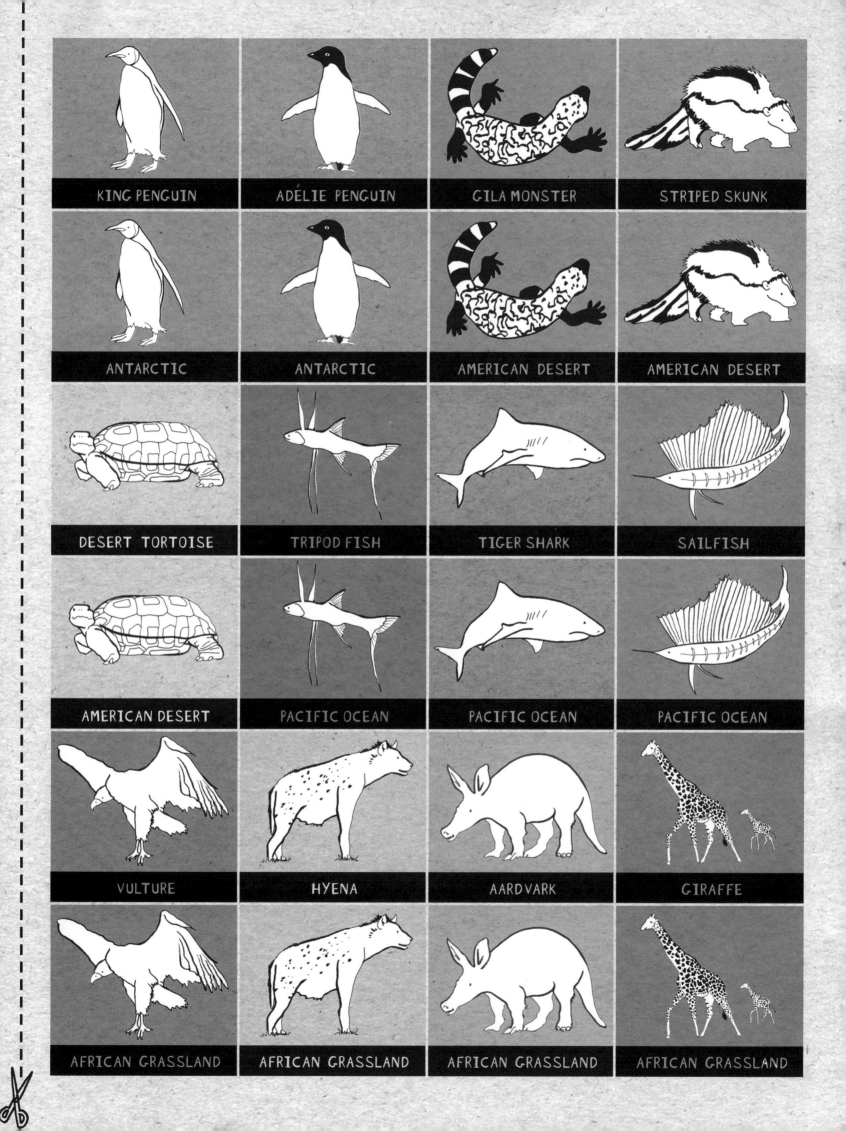

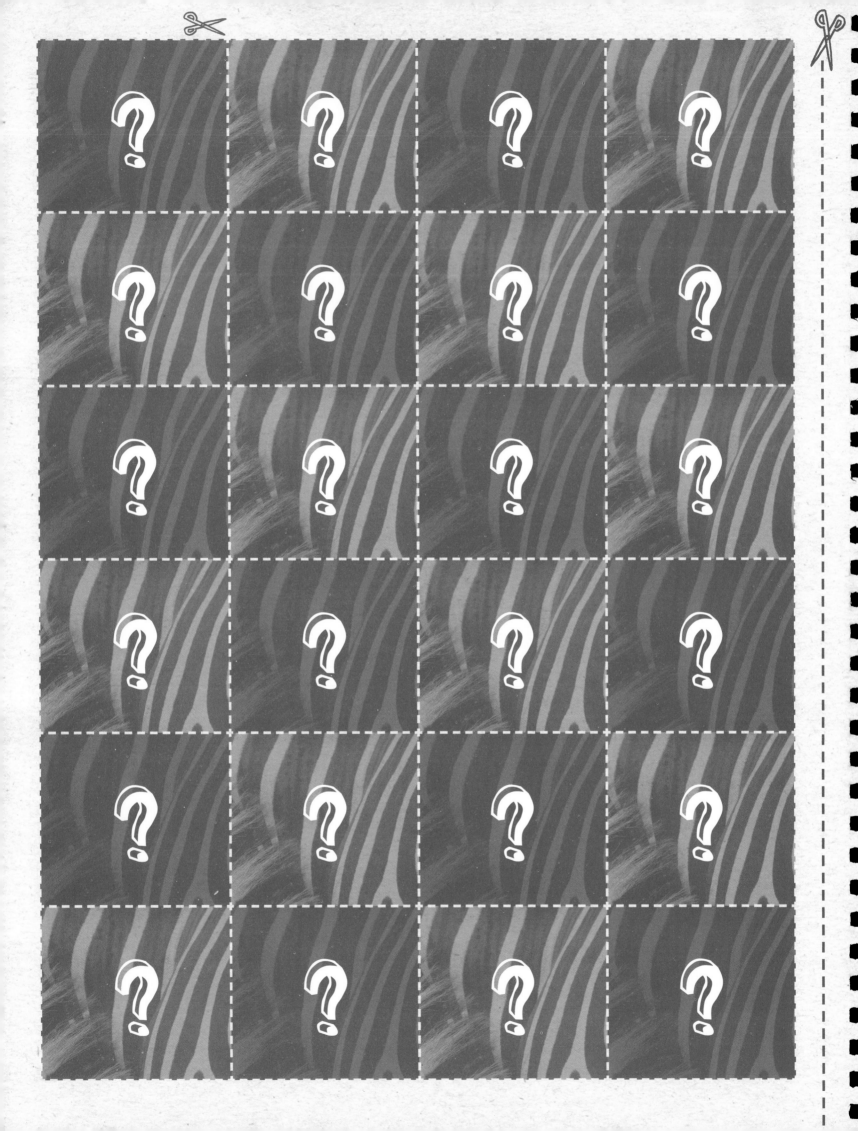

Nature Comes to Town

Color in the picture of nighttime in the city
to see who is out and about in the dark.

1 – Green
2 – Dark green
3 – Gray
4 – Dark blue
5 – Purple
6 – Brown

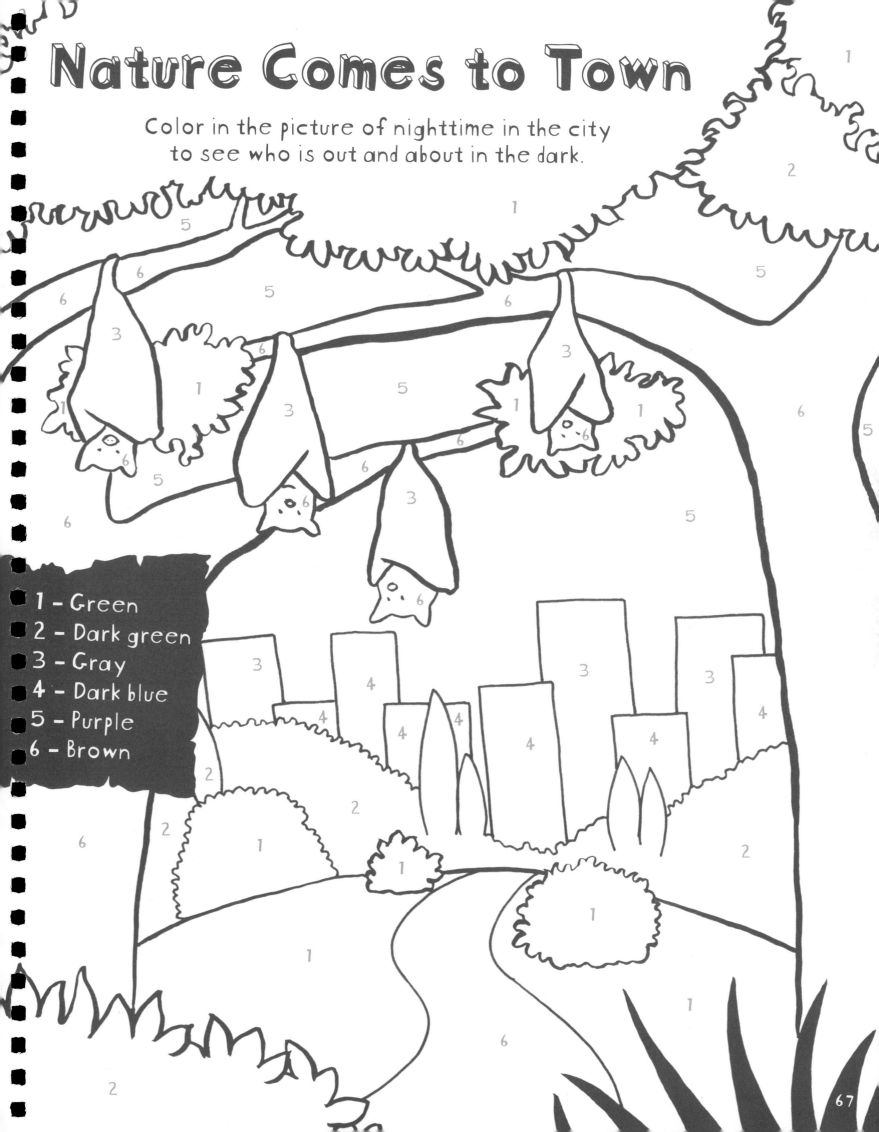

Up on the Rooftops

Use stickers to finish this picture of animals
you might find up on the rooftops of a city.

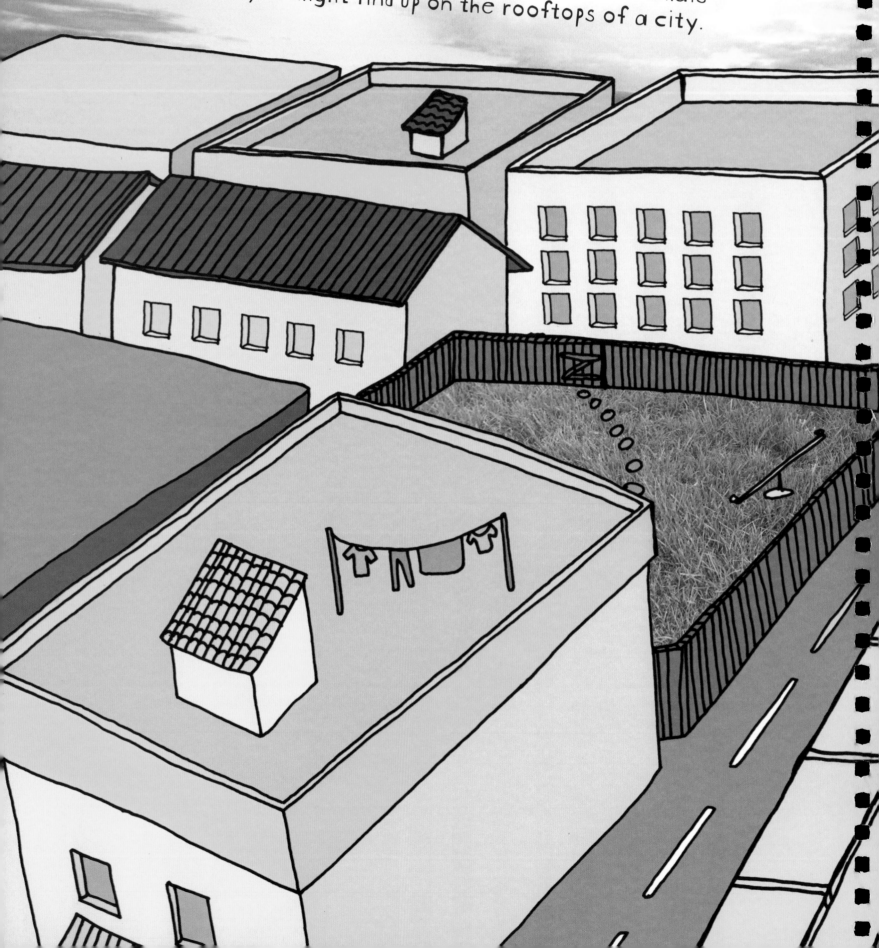

Rooftop Garden

Create your own city rooftop garden using crayons and stickers.

Watch Nature Happen

Color in the cartoon strip showing a little
seed growing into a flower.

What do you think the
bees are saying?

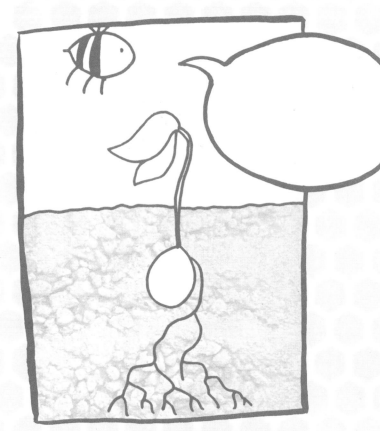

Perfect Petals

Many artists have been inspired by flowers, and you will often see pictures of them on stained-glass windows.

Color in this stained-glass window picture to make your own version.

Grow Your Own ART

Cut out a pretty pot decoration to fit around a little plant pot, and add some cute plant critters, too. They can be threaded onto kebab or plant sticks and popped into your pot.

PLANT POT DECORATION

1. Carefully cut around the decoration, and ask an adult to cut along the slit on one side.

2. Fit the decoration around your pot and slip the tab into the slit at the back to hold it in place.

STICK CRITTERS

1. Carefully cut out the critters.

2. Pierce through the card and thread a stick through each critter, as shown above.

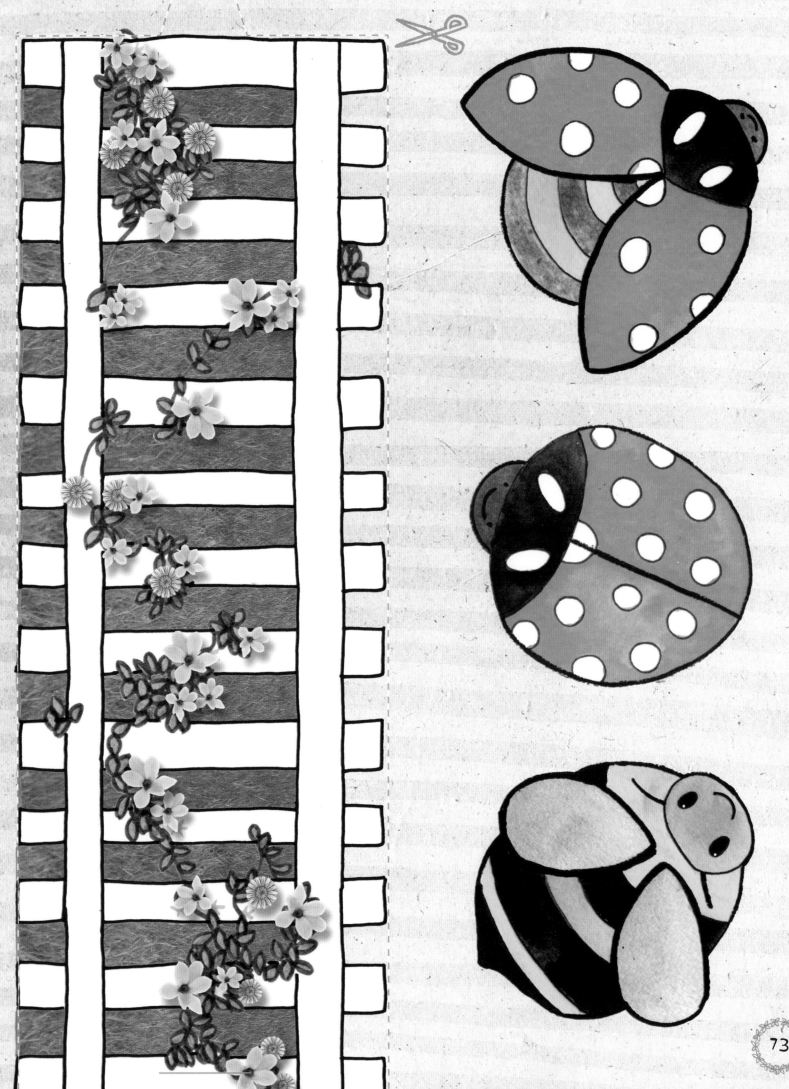

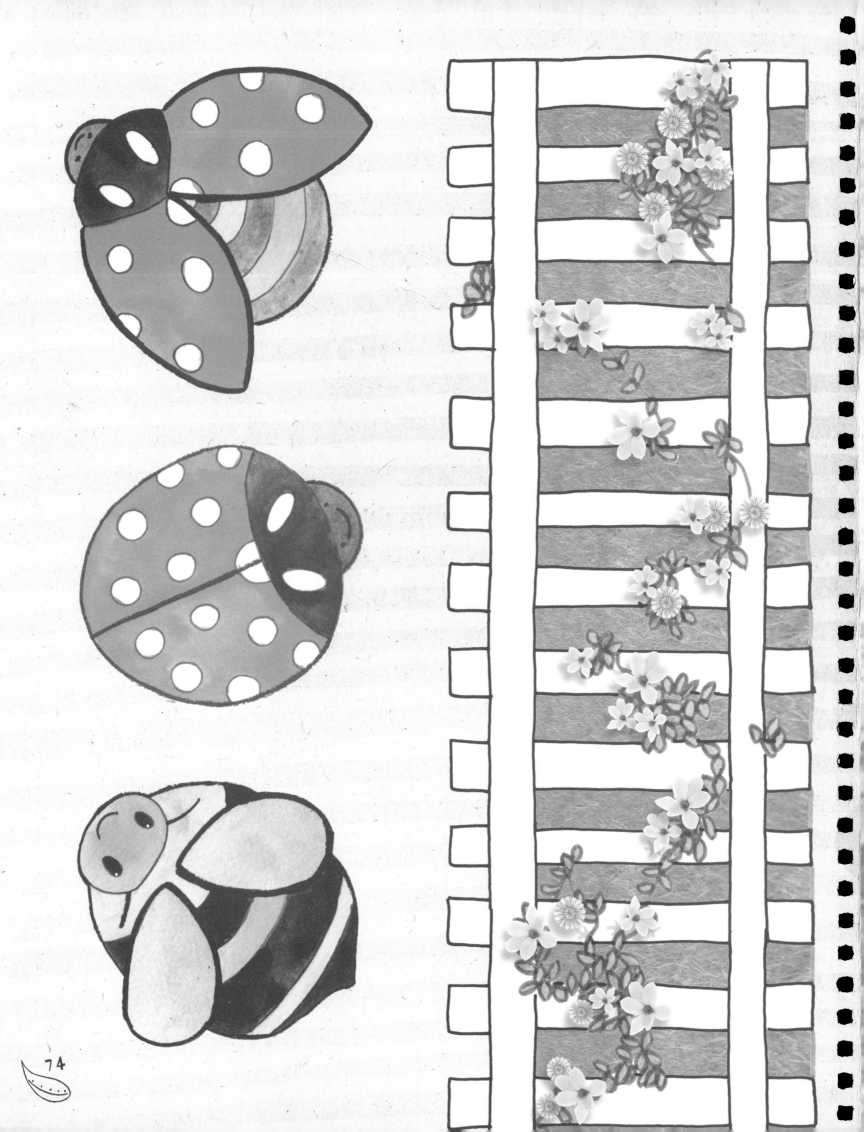

74

Buzz Buzz Puzzle

Can you match up the bee pairs and find the odd bee out?

Bees collect a sweet liquid called nectar from flowers. They use the nectar to make honey.

The bees carry pollen between the flowers they visit. Plants need pollen to make new seeds.

A

B

C

D

E

F

G

The answers are on page 80.

Thanks a bunch!

Make a pretty bunch of paper
flowers and put them on display
in an empty vase or jar.

1. Cut out the flowers,
flower centers, and
leaves on page 77.

2. Then choose a flower
and a flower center
to glue together.

3. Tape or glue on a plant
stick at the back of each
flower and wrap a leaf
around each stick, gluing
it in place.

You've completed your book. Well done!
You deserve an official award.

Fill this in, cut it out, and hang it on your wall.

The Academy of Wildlife Experts

We are delighted to award this certificate to

____

for being such a

Wildlife Genius!

BY ORDER OF

Anne Elephant and G. Raffe

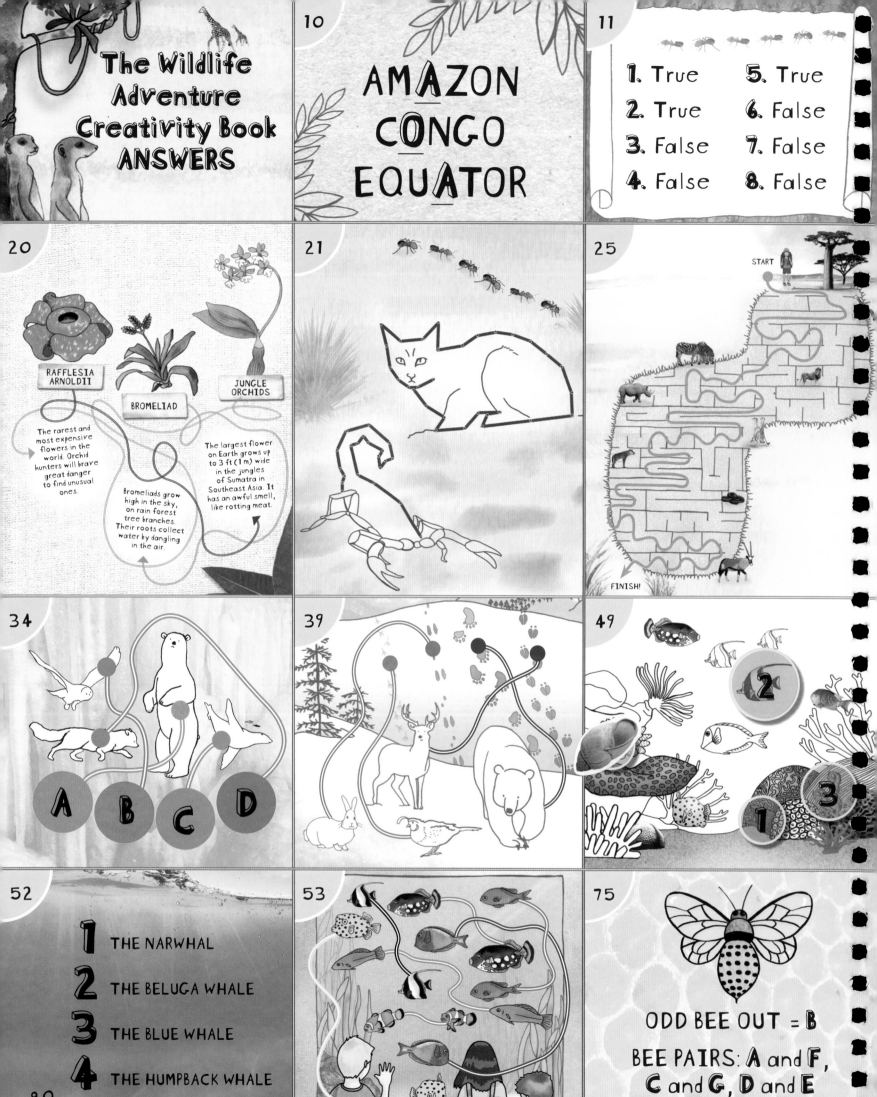

The Wildlife
Adventure
Creativity Book
ANSWERS

10

AMAZON
CONGO
EQUATOR

11

1. True   5. True
2. True   6. False
3. False   7. False
4. False   8. False

20

RAFFLESIA ARNOLDII

BROMELIAD

JUNGLE ORCHIDS

The rarest and most expensive flowers in the world. Orchid hunters will brave great danger to find unusual ones.

The largest flower on Earth grows up to 3 ft (1 m) wide in the jungles of Sumatra in Southeast Asia. It has an awful smell, like rotting meat.

Bromeliads grow high in the sky, on rain forest tree branches. Their roots collect water by dangling in the air.

21

25

START

FINISH!

34

A   B   C   D

39

49

2

1   3

52

1 THE NARWHAL

2 THE BELUGA WHALE

3 THE BLUE WHALE

4 THE HUMPBACK WHALE

80

53

75

ODD BEE OUT = B

BEE PAIRS: A and F,
C and G, D and E